LIVING WITH
LEUKAEMIA

Patsy Westcott

WAYLAND

Titles in the series

Living with Asthma

Living with Blindness

Living with Cerebral Palsy

Living with Deafness

Living with Diabetes

Living with Down's Syndrome

Living with Epilepsy

Living with Leukaemia

Editor: Carron Brown
Cover design: Steve Wheele Design
Book design: Peter Laws
Picture researcher: Gina Brown

First published in 1999 by Wayland Publishers Ltd, 61 Western Road, Hove,
East Sussex, BN3 1JD, England

Find Wayland on the Internet at http://www.wayland.co.uk

British Library Cataloguing in Publication Data
Westcott, Patsy
  Living with Leukaemia
  1. Leukaemia in children – Popular works –Juvenile literature
  2. Leukaemia in children – Case studies – Juvenile literature
  I. Title
  618.9'2'99419

ISBN 0 7502 2518 1

Printed and bound by G. Canale & C.S.p.A., Turin, Italy

The author would like to thank Felicity Hanlon of CLIC; Ken Campbell of the
Leukaemia Research Fund and Simon Cotterill of the Sir James Spence Institute of
Child Health, University of Newcastle upon Tyne for their help.

Picture acknowledgements
Wayland Publishers Ltd would like to thank: Angela Hampton 11; Science Photo
Library/Dr Tony Brain 19 (left), /John Durham 19 (right), /Simon Fraser, Royal
Victoria Infirmary, Newcastle 16, /Will & Deni MacIntyre 10, /Ed Young 14 (top); Tony
Stone/Zigy Kaluzny *cover* (inset top), 18; Wayland photo library 8, 9. The remaining
photographs were taken by Martyn F. Chillmaid for Wayland Publishers Ltd.

The photographer, Martyn F. Chillmaid, would like to thank Church Hill Middle School
and St Bede's RC Middle School in Redditch for all their help.

The illustrations on pages 6 and 7 are by Michael Courtney.

Most of the people who have been photographed for this book are models.

The Leukaemia Research Fund has been consulted throughout the preparation of this book.

Contents

Meet Susie, Jack and Rosie

Susie is 14 years old. When Susie was 12, she had leukaemia, a type of cancer. Susie's leukaemia is in remission, which means that there are no more cancer cells in her blood. She has to go to the hospital for regular check-ups to make sure the leukaemia cells are not coming back. Susie's favourite school subject is art. She is very good at drawing and painting. When Susie leaves school, she would like to go to university to study art. In her spare time, she likes in-line skating and listening to music.

▷ After having treatment, Susie was able to do all the activities she likes again, like skating.

▷ Jack wants to be a footballer like his favourite players, when he grows older.

Jack is 10 years old. He lives with his parents and his brother Tim, who is 8 years old. When Jack was 9, he developed leukaemia and had to have treatment in hospital. The hospital was quite a long way from where Jack lives, so his mum and Tim came and stayed in a house nearby. Jack and Tim went to the hospital school. Jack is at home again now that his leukaemia is in remission, and he and Tim are back at their normal school. Jack likes yo-yos, playing on his computer and playing football with Tim. Jack and Tim want to be footballers when they grow up.

Rosie is 5 years old and has just started school. She lives with her parents, her brother Jake, who is 8, and her sister Chloe, who is 3. The doctor has just discovered that Rosie has leukaemia. She is being treated in hospital. Rosie likes ballet and playing with her cat, Leo.

◁ Rosie and her cat Leo before she went into hospital.

5

What is leukaemia?

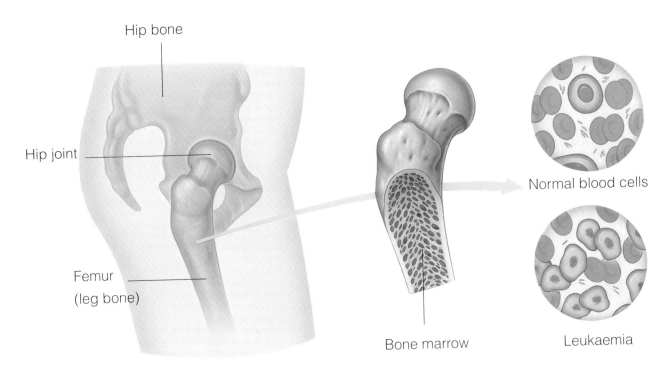

Hip bone

Hip joint

Femur
(leg bone)

Bone marrow

Normal blood cells

Leukaemia

Leukaemia is a type of cancer, an illness that happens when the cells in one part of your body start growing and dividing faster than normal. Doctors describe these abnormal cells as 'malignant' and if they are not treated, they can spread to other parts of the body.

Cancer can affect any part of the body. When cancer affects a solid body tissue, such as your muscles, your brain or your kidneys, the cancer cells stick together and form a lump called a tumour. Leukaemia is a cancer of the blood and the bone marrow, the soft, spongy material in the middle of your bones. The bone marrow is like a 'factory' where new blood cells are made.

△ This illustration shows the difference between bone marrow with leukaemic cells and with normal blood cells. Leukaemia means more white blood cells and fewer platelets in the blood.

In leukaemia, there are more white blood cells in the bone marrow than there should be and they are not fully developed like normal white blood cells. These leukaemic cells, as they are called, do not form a lump. Instead, they crowd the bone marrow and float around in the bloodstream.

Types of blood cell

The bone marrow makes three types of blood cell:
- red blood cells carry oxygen around your body;
- white blood cells fight the germs that cause coughs, colds and other infections;
- platelets help your blood to clot and prevent bleeding and bruising if you are injured.

When someone has leukaemia, the white leukaemic cells crowd out red cells and platelets, and the bone marrow is unable to make as many new cells as before.

▽ These are the different types of blood cell in your body.

Red blood cells

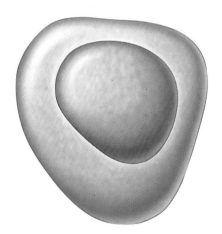

White blood cell

Platelets

Types of leukaemia

There are many different types of leukaemia. Rosie has acute leukaemia and Jack and Susie had this type of leukaemia, too. 'Acute' is a word doctors use to describe an illness or a symptom that develops suddenly and progresses fast. Adults and children can both develop leukaemia, but acute leukaemia is most common in children.

▽ Adults can get leukaemia, but they don't usually have the same types as children get.

Many people feel frightened when they hear the word 'leukaemia' because thirty years ago most children who had the illness used to die. Leukaemia is a very serious illness indeed if it is not treated. However, there are medicines available today that are very successful in treating the disease, and many children with acute leukaemia get better. In fact, seven out of ten children with leukaemia are completely cured. Unfortunately, some types of leukaemia are still hard to cure and so, sadly, despite being treated, a few children do not get better.

△ The most common age for children to develop leukaemia is between 2 and 5 years old.

Why do some people develop leukaemia?

▽ This woman is having an ultrasound scan to check the health of her baby. Leukaemia may begin when a baby is still in its mother's the womb.

The exact causes of leukaemia are not known. Acute leukaemia starts with a mistake in a single white cell. This mistake gets copied over and over again as the cell divides, until there are billions of leukaemic cells in the bone marrow and the blood. It's a bit like a spelling mistake in a story that is copied many times. Every time the story is copied, the mistake is repeated until there are a lot of copies, all with the same mistake.

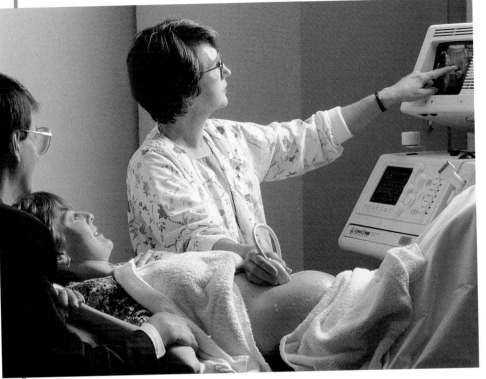

Scientists are trying to find out why the mistake, called a mutation, happens in the cell in the first place. They have many different ideas. Some think that an infection or a virus causes some children to develop a rare reaction that causes the cell to change. Some think that the cell becomes damaged if a baby is exposed to X-rays or certain chemicals while he or she is still in the womb, or after birth.

Some scientists are trying to find out whether being exposed to electromagnetic fields from overhead electric power lines, and from substations where electricity is made, might cause damage to the cell. Others are studying the part that may be played by the genes, the material in your cells that governs the way your body behaves. When scientists discover what causes leukaemia, other scientists will be to design even better drugs and other treatments to help cure it.

Despite all this research, no one really knows what causes leukaemia. However, we do know that you cannot catch it from someone who has got it, you cannot give it to someone else if you have it and it is not caused by anything someone with leukaemia has said or done.

△ Leukaemia may be a disease that is passed on through the genes of a family.

What are the symptoms of leukaemia?

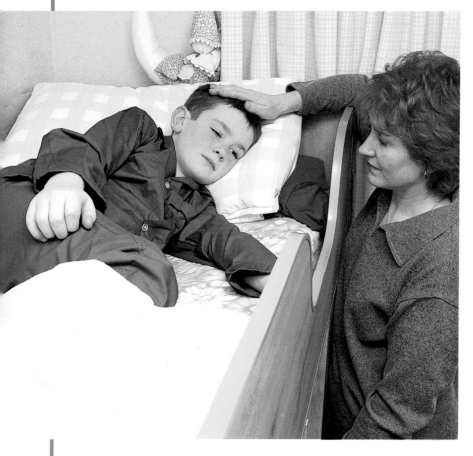

△ Leukaemia made Jack feel tired and weak.

Jack always felt ill. He kept getting infections, such as colds, coughs or sore throats, one after the other. Jack also felt tired a lot. When he got home from school, Jack would go straight up to his bedroom and lie down. He told his mum he felt floppy and complained of pains in his arms and legs. He didn't like walking to school any more because his legs ached so much.

One day, Jack noticed blood on his toothbrush when he cleaned his teeth. He told his mum.

Jack also noticed that if he got even a little knock, a big bruise would come up on his skin. His mum thought he looked pale and ill. Jack was fed up because he felt unwell all the time.

The illnesses Jack experienced are typical of leukaemia. However, there is no reason to think you have leukaemia if you sometimes feel tired or get a cold or the odd bruise.

There are two reasons why leukaemia causes these symptoms. Firstly, the leukaemic cells are dividing so fast that they crowd the bone marrow 'factory', making it impossible for it to make the right amount of normal blood cells. Secondly, the leukaemic cells travel in the blood to other parts of the body and stop them from working properly.

People with leukaemia feel tired and weak because their bone marrow is making too few red blood cells. This results in a condition called anaemia, which causes tiredness, breathlessness and pale skin.

▽ Jack felt so tired that he didn't even want to play football with his brother.

Pain in the bones is caused by the bone marrow becoming crowded with leukaemic cells. Bruising and bleeding (for example, the bleeding from the gums that Jack noticed) happen because the bone marrow cannot make enough platelets.

The frequent infections people get when they have leukaemia happen because there are not enough healthy white blood cells.

Rosie's tests

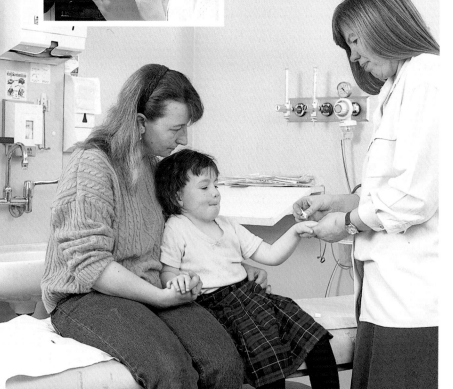

▽ Scientists can look closely at someone's blood cells through a microscope.

Rosie's mum was worried about Rosie's health, so she took her to the doctor. The doctor did some tests to try to help her work out what was wrong with Rosie. She used a needle to prick the back of Rosie's hand and draw out a small amount of blood. It didn't hurt because she put a special cream on Rosie's skin to stop her from feeling the prick.

Rosie's blood sample was sent to a hospital laboratory. A machine was used to count the numbers of white cells, red cells and platelets in Rosie's blood. This is called a blood count. Some of Rosie's blood was put on a glass slide and a scientist looked at it through a microscope. The scientist looking at Rosie's blood could tell she had leukaemia because he saw a lot of unhealthy white cells and too few red cells and platelets.

◁ The doctor took a sample of Rosie's blood so a scientist could examine it.

▷ Rosie's doctor came round to the house to tell her parents that Rosie had leukaemia.

Another test used to diagnose leukaemia is called a bone marrow biopsy. This is when a small amount of bone marrow is drawn from inside the hip bone using a hollow needle. Before Rosie had her bone marrow biopsy, a doctor injected a special medicine called an anaesthetic. This made her go to sleep for a while and stopped her feeling pain. Sometimes, the anaesthetic is a gas which you breathe in through a mask. When the doctor looked at Rosie's bone marrow under the microscope, he could tell what sort of leukaemia she had.

When the hospital told Rosie's doctor that she had leukaemia, she went to Rosie's house and told her mum and dad. Rosie and her parents went straight to the hospital with the doctor.

My tests

'When the doctor said she was going to do some tests, I felt a bit scared. She was really nice and told me that they would help find out why I was ill. I had medicines that stopped me hurting during the tests, so I really didn't need to be scared.'

Treating leukaemia

Jack, Susie and Rosie all had to take special drugs to kill the leukaemic cells in their blood and bone marrow. This treatment is called chemotherapy. Several drugs are usually used to make sure all the leukaemic cells are killed. Drugs can be taken by mouth as tablets or pills, but usually they are injected or given through a drip, a bag of medicine that can be pumped straight into the bloodstream.

▽ This boy with leukaemia is being given medicine through a drip.

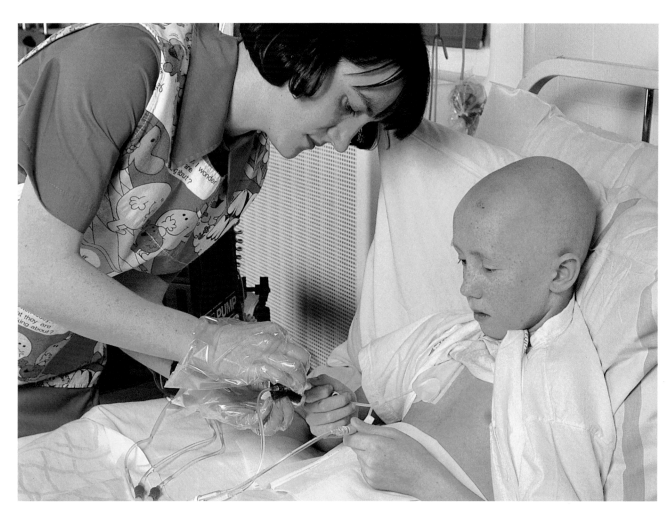

> Jack can still play
football with his wiggly
line in place. He keeps
it hidden under a long-
sleeved top. Jack
needs the line in place
for occasional follow-up
treatment at the
hospital.

Often a tube that goes straight into a vein is put into the
chest or the groin. The proper name for this is a venous
line, although many children with leukaemia call it a
'wiggly line'. It is put in under anaesthetic so the person
does not feel anything. At the end of the line, a little
tube pokes out of the skin with a rubber stopper on the
end. When the doctors or nurses want to give the person
drugs or take blood, they can use the line so the person
does not have to have so many injections.

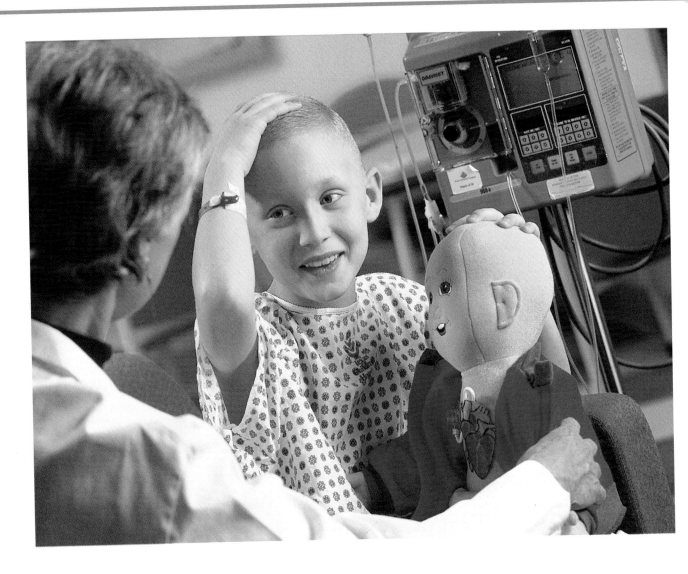

The drugs used to treat leukaemia can sometimes make people feel quite ill. They may feel sick and tired, get a funny taste in their mouth, develop mouth ulcers or a sore stomach. Very often their hair falls out. These side-effects happen because the chemotherapy drugs do not just kill unhealthy leukaemic cells, they also kill healthy cells like those in the skin and the hair. Many side-effects can be prevented, for example, a doctor can give people a medicine to stop them feeling sick. However, these side-effects always go away once treatment is stopped.

△ This girl has lost her hair because of chemotherapy treatment. It will grow back again when the treatment is finished.

Sometimes radiotherapy is used. This treatment uses X-rays to kill leukaemic cells. After treatment has finished, the child may feel tired for a few days or weeks.

Often, treatments such as chemotherapy and radiotherapy make the leukaemia go into remission. Sometimes the leukaemia goes away but then comes back again. This is called relapsing. If someone relapses, he or she can sometimes have a bone marrow transplant. This replaces the unhealthy bone marrow cells with healthy ones. The healthy cells are taken from the bone marrow of a relative or someone else with cells that match those of the person with leukaemia. This person is called a bone marrow donor.

▽ When seen under a microscope, the blood of someone with leukaemia has a large number of abnormal white blood cells.

Healthy cells

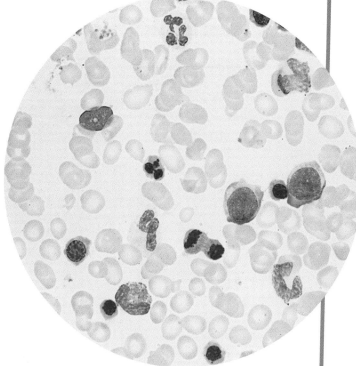

Leukaemic cells

Rosie goes to hospital

Rosie has to stay in hospital while she has chemotherapy. The hospital has nurses and doctors who are experienced in treating children with cancer. The hospital is in a different town from the one where she normally lives with her family, so Rosie's mum is staying in the hospital with her. Her brother and sister, Jake and Chloe, are staying at home with their dad and their nan. They visit her as often as they can.

In hospital

'I don't mind being in hospital too much because my mum is with me too.'

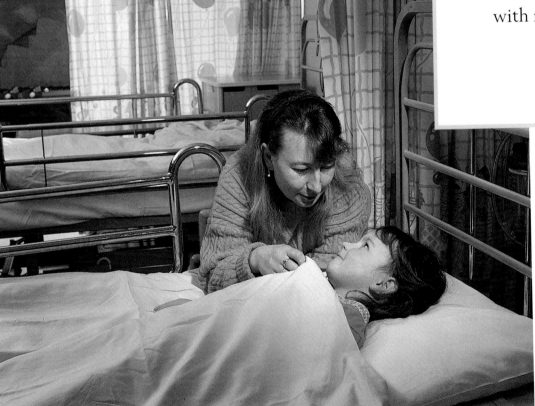

◁ Rosie's mum tucks her up in bed every night at the hospital.

△ Rosie has a lot of toys to play with at the hospital.

In hospital, Rosie has many toys to play with. Someone called a play therapist often comes and plays with her or reads her a story. On days when she feels a bit better, she goes to the hospital school. Rosie does not mind being in hospital too much, but she misses her family and her cat, Leo.

Jake and Chloe miss Rosie and they worry about her. Chloe draws a card and sends it to Rosie every day. Jake and Chloe do not like staying at home without their mum. They speak to their mum on the phone and she comes back to see them, but sometimes she seems more worried about Rosie and spends most of the time talking to their nan. This makes Jake and Chloe cross and sometimes they even feel jealous of Rosie. They feel left out, because people have bought Rosie a lot of presents. Sometimes they feel that people care more about Rosie than they do about them.

▷ Jake and Chloe like having their nan to look after them, but they miss having Rosie and their mum around.

Jack and his friends

Last year, Jack had to stay in hospital but now his leukaemia is in remission and he's back home. Jack has to have treatment for another two years to make sure the leukaemic cells stay away for good. He has to go to the hospital for this but he does not have to stay. Instead, he has his treatment in an out-patients clinic.

Sometimes after a treatment, Jack's white blood cell count is low, which means that he has trouble fighting off infections like colds. If one of his friends has an infection when his blood count is low, Jack has to be careful to stay away. Jack's mum takes his temperature every day. If it is higher than normal, it could be a sign that he is developing an infection.

▽ Jack is happier now he's in remission and he can play with his friends.

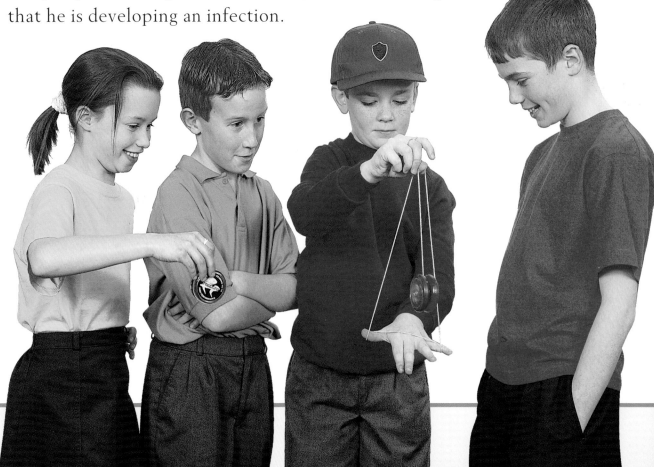

▷ Jack still gets tired during his day at school.

Understanding leukaemia

'Some of my friends kept away from me when I first came back. I think they felt embarrassed. When I talked to them about my leukaemia, it helped them to understand.'

Jack has gone back to school. At first, he just went in the mornings but as he began to feel stronger, he started staying all day. Sometimes, he feels tired and has to go home.

Jack was a bit worried about going back to school. He lost his hair while he was having chemotherapy and sometimes he wears a hat. Although Jack's hair is growing back, he was worried that other children would stare or make fun of him.

Jack's friends are pleased that he's back home, but some of them felt embarrassed and did not know what to say to him. The community cancer nurse visited the school and told Jack's class all about leukaemia. Jack told them about his leukaemia, too, and showed them the end of his venous line. Once Jack's friends understood about his leukaemia they did not feel embarrassed any more.

Susie is sad

Susie's leukaemia is better now. She does not need to have any more treatment, but she still has to go to the hospital for check-ups.

◁ Susie and her friend Emma spent a lot of happy times together.

Susie belongs to a group for teenagers who have cancer or who used to have it . Her special friend at the group was a girl called Emma who had leukaemia, too, but it was a different kind to Susie's leukaemia. Susie and Emma enjoyed going shopping, or to the cinema and sometimes they slept at each other's houses. One day, Emma told Susie that her leukaemia had come back and she had to go back into hospital for more treatment. Sadly the treatment did not work. Emma's leukaemia became so bad that she was not able to fight it any more and she died.

Susie felt terrible when Emma died. She felt very sad and kept on crying. She was also frightened in case her leukaemia came back too, even though she knew it was a different type of leukaemia to Emma's. Susie also felt angry that Emma had died. Sometimes, she felt cross with the doctors and nurses. Sometimes, she even felt cross with Emma.

Emma's mum invited Susie to come to Emma's funeral. Emma's family and many of her friends were there. Everybody was very sad but after the funeral they all went back to Emma's house for tea and talked about Emma. They remembered all the things Emma had done. Although Susie still feels sad, she also remembers all the good times they had together. She feels glad that she knew Emma.

Being strong

'I think the fight against leukaemia has made me stronger. If I can come through this, I can come through anything.'

▷ Before Susie went home, Emma's mum gave Susie a necklace that belonged to Emma. Susie often wears it and thinks about her.

25

Looking to the future

Susie, Jack and Rosie are just like you, except that they have or have had leukaemia. Apart from having treatment and having to stay in hospital sometimes, their lives are just like yours. They still have fun with their friends, go to school, and enjoy having hobbies and doing all the kinds of things you and your friends like doing.

▽ Jack is glad to be back home with his family.

Jack, Susie and Rosie know leukaemia can be tough both for people who have the disease and for their friends and families. Treatment can sometimes cause side-effects long after the cancer has gone away. Occasionally, children who have had leukaemia have some problems with their memory. Sometimes, they may start to develop into adults later than other children, and sometimes when they grow up they may not be able to have children of their own. The good news is that treatments are getting better all the time and most children who have had leukaemia will not have these problems.

△ Susie keeps in touch with other children and support groups all over the world using the Internet.

Today, many children who have had leukaemia can expect to grow up fit and healthy. They might go to university, have jobs, get married and have families, just like you. There are people who have had leukaemia doing all sorts of jobs and living all kinds of lives.

Jack, Susie and Rosie are determined not to let leukaemia beat them. They do not want you to feel sorry for them. They do want you to understand and to recognize that they are still the same people they were before they developed leukaemia, so they can get on with their lives.

Getting help

△ Susie likes to talk about her time with leukaemia with other children who have had the disease.

There are many organizations for children and adults who have leukaemia or other forms of cancer. Some of them provide help, advice and support for people with any kind of cancer. Others provide help and advice just on leukaemia. Many hospitals provide books, videos and other information or run their own support groups.

Some organizations are for adults and children with cancer. Others are just for children or teenagers. Many publish leaflets, books and videos about cancer or leukaemia. Some provide services like 'homes from home' where children with cancer and their families can stay while they are having treatment. This is especially helpful as treatment may have to be done at a hospital some way from their homes. Other organizations provide information on services in a particular town, city or area.

The Leukaemia Research Fund raises funds for research into all forms of leukaemia and cancers of the blood, and can provide leaflets about these diseases. You can contact them by writing to 43 Great Ormond Street, London, WC1N 3JJ, or by phone (0171 405 0101), or you can also look at their website (www.leukaemia-research.org.uk).

CLIC (Cancer and Leukaemia in Childhood) provides a range of practical help for children with cancer and their families, as well as funding vital equipment and resources in hospital. CLIC's services include homes from home where the family can live during the child's hospital treatment. It also funds CLIC nurses and community cancer nurses, who work with children and their families at home and in hospital, runs an ambulance service to take children to and from hospital, provides play therapists for children during hospital visits or stays, and provides other practical help and information for children with cancer and their families. Its address is 12–13 King Square, Bristol, BS2 8JH. Tel: 0117 924 8844.

△ Most organizations hold fund-raising events to help fund resources and research into the treatment and causes of leukaemia.

Sargent Cancer Care for Children supports children and their families at home and in hospital from the day of diagnosis. It provides counselling advice and financial assistance to families in need. Sargent Social Workers are based at all the major cancer centres in the UK. You can contact them at 14 Abingdon Road, London W8 6AF. Tel: 0171 565 5100.

Glossary

Bloodstream The movement of blood around your body.

Bone marrow The soft, spongy material in the centre of your bones.

Cells Tiny parts of any living thing – plants, animals or human. Your skin, your hair, your nails, your blood, your bones, in fact all the parts of your body are all made up of cells.

Chemotherapy Treatment with cancer killing drugs.

Clinic Part of a building or hospital where people go to have special treatment or advice.

Diagnose To work out what sort of disease someone has by looking at their symptoms and carrying out tests.

Electromagnetic field A kind of energy that is both electric and magnetic. This energy exists around electric cables containing a strong electric current.

Infection An illness that is passed on from one person to another.

Laboratory A kind of workshop where scientists do experiments.

Malignant Cells that have cancer. The cells are able to spread to other parts of the body.

Platelets Small blood cells that help the blood to clot, and prevent bleeding and bruising.

Red blood cells Cells that carry oxygen.

Relapse When the disease comes back after appearing to go away.

Remission When the abnormal cancer cells can no longer be seen in the blood.

Side-effects The other effects of using a drug, which are usually unpleasant.

Symptom A sign that someone looks for to recognize an illness.

Tissue Parts of your body around your bones, such as muscle.

Tumour A swollen mass of diseased cells in body tissue.

Vein A part of the body that blood moves through.

Virus The cause of an infection.

White blood cells Blood cells that help the body fight off infections

Further information

Books for children
Fighting the Big C by Sarah Palmer (CLIC, Bristol, 1994)
Jenny has Leukaemia by Anne Nicholson and Janice Thompson. Sponsored by and available from Sargent Cancer Care for Children (address on page 29).
Why am I going to Hospital? by Carole Livingston (Angus and Robertson, 1983) For readers of 5 years old and up.
Why, Charlie Brown, Why? by C.Shultz (Ravette, 1990)

Books for older readers
When Someone has a Very Serious Illness by M. Heegaard (Woodland Press, 1991)

Videos
Why, Charlie Brown, Why? features well-known *Peanuts* characters to illustrate what happens when a friend develops leukaemia. Available from the American Cancer Society and some hospital units.
Somewhere Over the Rainbow from the Malcolm Sargent Social Work Office at the Royal Victoria Infirmary, Newcastle upon Tyne NE1 4LP.

Websites
Children's cancer web
www.ncl.ac.uk/child-health/guides/guide2.htm
The Leukaemia Research Fund has published patient information and leaflets that you can read on:
www.leukaemia.demon.co.uk/patinfo.htm
Guide to Internet resources for cancer
www.ncl.ac.uk/child-health/guides/clinks1.htm

Index

Numbers in **bold** refer to pictures as well as text.